D0764220

DAKOTA FANNING

Clare Hibbert

SEA-TO-SEA

Mankato Collingwood London

This edition first published in 2013 by
Sea-to-Sea Publications
Distributed by Black Rabbit Books
P.O. Box 3263, Mankato, Minnesota 56002

Printed in the United States of America, North Mankato, MN

9 8 7 6 5 4 3 2

Published by arrangement with the Watts Publishing Group Ltd, London.

Library of Congress Cataloging-in-Publication Data

Hibbert, Clare, 1970–
 Dakota Fanning / written by Clare Hibbert.
    p. cm. -- (Teen stars)
 Includes index.
 ISBN 978-1-59771-413-6 (hardcover, library bound)
 1. Fanning, Dakota, 1994---Juvenile literature. 2. Actors--United States--Biography--Juvenile
literature. I. Title.
 PN2287.F325H53 2013
 791.4302'8'092--dc23
 [B]
                                    2012002535

Series Editor: Adrian Cole
Art Direction: Peter Scoulding
Design: Simon Borrough
Picture Research: Diana Morris

Acknowledgements:
Matt Baron/BEI/Rex Features: 22.
Beretta/Sims/Rex Features: 28.
EdStock/iStockphoto: 5.
Everett/Rex Features: 10, 12, 21.
Sara Jaye/Rex Features: 25.
Henry Lamb/BEI/Rex Features: 29.
Jamie McCarthy/WireImages/Getty Images: 14.
MGM/Everett/Rex Features: 13.
NBCU Photobank/Rex Features: 6.
New Line/Everett/Rex Features: 8, 9.
Masatoshi Okauchi /Rex Features: 17.
Paramount/Everett/Rex Features: 18.
Photos 12/Alamy: 23.
Jo Seer/Shutterstock: front cover.
Startraks Photo/Rex Features: 15, 19.
Casey Steele/Getty Images: 27.
TM & © 20th Century Fox/Everett/Rex Features: 20.

*Every attempt has been made to clear copyright. Should there be any inadvertent omission
please apply to the publisher for rectification.*

RD/6000006415/001
May 2012

Contents

Words highlighted in the text can be found in the glossary.

Child Star

Dakota Fanning is an amazing actress. By the age of 17, she had appeared in more than 30 movies, including *I Am Sam*, *War of the Worlds*, *Charlotte's Web*, and *The Runaways*.

Dakota starred in her first Hollywood movie at the age of seven—and she has never looked back. She has made films with some of the biggest names in the business, and earned millions of dollars in the process.

Despite her extraordinary success, Dakota has kept her feet on the ground. She may be pretty and sweet, but she

"One of my favorite things about doing movies is that you get to do different things you'd never do in real life."

also has genuine talent. Thanks to her own hard work, she has matured into a serious, super-versatile actress.

At the age of eight, Dakota became the youngest person ever to be **nominated** for a Screen Actors Guild Award. It was for her supporting role in *I Am Sam*.

Early Years

Hannah Dakota Fanning was born on February 23, 1994, in Conyers, Georgia. Dakota was four when her sister, Elle, was born. When Dakota was five, the local kids' drama club saw her talent and advised her parents to talk to an agency.

Dakota appeared in the **pilot** for *The Fighting Fitzgeralds* in 2001.

Dakota didn't have to wait long before she picked up the star role in a nationwide TV commercial. Dakota, her mom, dad, and sister all moved to Los Angeles, California.

Dakota's parents, Steve and Joy, had backgrounds in sports, not drama. Her mom was a professional tennis player and her dad was a baseball player for the St. Louis Cardinals.

"ER was one of my favorites. I played a car accident victim who has leukemia. I got to wear a neck brace and nose tubes for the two days I worked."

Dakota was soon making guest appearances in all kinds of top TV shows. She had roles in *ER, CSI: Crime Scene Investigation, The Practice, Spin City,* and *Ally McBeal.*

Big Break

Dakota's big movie break came in 2001, when she was chosen to play the daughter in *I Am Sam*. Sam was a single parent with learning difficulties. He was played by Sean Penn. In the film Sam fights for custody of his daughter.

Dakota snuggles up to her screen dad, actor Sean Penn, in *I Am Sam*.

Laura Dern and Sean Penn starred in *I Am Sam*, but Dakota was the real star of the movie.

The character Dakota played was named Lucy Diamond Dawson. She won the Best Young Actor Award from the Broadcast Film Critics Association for her performance.

Dakota's real-life little sister, Elle, had her first movie part in *I Am Sam*, playing a younger version of Lucy.

"In the happy scenes, there were really fun times. Sean would say really funny stuff because he likes to improv[ise]. I would want to laugh, but you are not allowed to do that during the take."

9

Taken

Film director **Steven Spielberg** was impressed by Dakota in *I Am Sam*. He cast her to star in a miniseries he was producing for the SyFy Channel, called *Taken*.

Spielberg's *E.T. the Extra-Terrestrial* is the first movie Dakota remembers watching. Other films that he's directed include *Raiders of the Lost Ark, Jurassic Park*, and *War Horse*.

In *Taken*, Dakota (right) plays Allie, the on-screen daughter of Lisa Clarke (left), played by Emily Bergl.

Taken, which first aired in December 2002, went on to win an Emmy Award. The series was about alien experiments on humans, and it focused on three families. Dakota played Allie Keys, a girl who was part human and part alien.

66It's just such an honor to say that I was in something by Steven Spielberg. I feel so blessed I got to meet such great people, and I got to go to a beautiful place, Vancouver, and I had a great time.99

Major Movies

The years 2002 and 2003 were busy for Dakota. She starred in four major Hollywood movies—*Trapped, Hansel and Gretel, Dr. Seuss' The Cat In The Hat*, and *Uptown Girls*.

Dakota, Mike Myers, and Spencer Breslin jump on a sofa in *Dr. Seuss' The Cat In The Hat*.

In the exciting thriller *Trapped*, Dakota played a kidnap victim with asthma. The other actors were sometimes so in awe of her that they forgot their own lines!

12

In *Hansel and Gretel*, Dakota played Katie, a modern-day girl listening to the Brothers Grimm fairy tale.

When Dakota was still only eight years old, she played Sally in *Dr. Seuss' The Cat In The Hat*. The movie starred zany Mike Myers as the cat. She also appeared in *Uptown Girls* with Brittany Murphy, playing an uptight little rich kid, Ray.

"I like everything perfect. Everything has to be neat. I make my bed every morning, everything's perfect. My shoes are all arranged. It's sad. I'm a little like Ray, a little bit."

Dakota stars alongside Brittany Murphy in *Uptown Girls*.

Family Support

Dakota knows she is lucky to have such supportive parents. They believed in her enough to move their family all the way from Georgia to California, where she had the chance to become an actress.

Since then, they've continued to help her to stay grounded, while allowing her to become independent. Both Dakota and her sister were still expected to do chores and help out around the house.

25

Elle (left) sits alongside her big sister at a fashion show in 2012.

Dakota's success inspired Elle to become an actress, too. Elle's movies include *Babel, Somewhere,* and *We Bought a Zoo.* She has acted alongside Brad Pitt, Matt Damon, and Scarlett Johansson.

"My parents wouldn't allow me to get above myself—ever. They never pushed me into acting. They just want me to do whatever makes me happy. If I had chosen something else, they would have been just as supportive."

Dakota with her mom Joy, in 2011.

Thrills
& Spills

In 2004, Dakota played a kidnap victim for the second time (the first was in *Trapped*). As schoolgirl Pita in *Man on Fire*, she melted the heart of her grumpy bodyguard Creasy, played by Denzel Washington.

The following year, Dakota was able to work with top director Steven Spielberg again when he made his epic film *War of the Worlds*. Not only that, but Tom Cruise costarred as her dad!

Dakota won a Saturn Award in recognition of her amazing performance as Rachel Ferrier in *War of the Worlds*.

"When I go on a movie set, I'm learning about movies. I learned 100 lessons a day from Steven [Spielberg]. I always think I might not have this opportunity again, so I try to cram a lot of information into my brain."

From left, Kathleen Kennedy **(producer)**, Steven Spielberg (director), Dakota, and actor Tom Cruise—part of the cast and crew on *War of the Worlds*.

Children's Classic

Dakota continued her successful movie career in 2006. She played farmer's daughter Fern Arable in *Charlotte's Web*, a dramatization of the classic children's novel by E. B. White.

Dakota as Fern Arable washes Wilbur the pig.

The *Charlotte's Web* cast included some of Hollywood's biggest names, but most were contributing only their voices. Julia Roberts had the part of Charlotte, and Steve Buscemi was Wilbur. Other animal parts were voiced by Oprah Winfrey, John Cleese, Kathy Bates, and Robert Redford.

Dakota at the **premiere** of *Charlotte's Web*.

Dakota was a little embarrassed to discover that she was a bigger box-office draw than Julia Roberts. "I don't think of myself that way. When people say that, it's really nice, but I don't even think that's true," she said modestly.

Dakota's sister, Elle, filmed some scenes for *Charlotte's Web*, but they were not included in the final version of the movie. She played Fern's future granddaughter.

Two Runaways

As she entered teenage life, Dakota began to take on more mature roles. These cast her as older characters and dealt with tougher issues.

The Secret Life of Bees was heartwarming— but it had a serious message, too. Dakota played a runaway taken in by three beekeeping sisters. They teach her a lot about acceptance and the civil rights movement.

"I think [The Secret Life of Bees] will be a great film for people my age to see who have never experienced any racial issues in their life."

Dakota in a scene from The Secret Life of Bees, which starred Queen Latifah as August Boatwright.

Dakota as Cherie Currie in *The Runaways*. The movie was Dakota's first real teen role.

"Because a lot of people don't know who Cherie is, this is going to be maybe their only way of knowing her story. It was exciting and a challenge, and I liked that."

The Runaways was different again. It was a true story about a 1970s girl band of the same name. Dakota played the troubled but feisty lead singer, Cherie Currie. The real Cherie sat with Dakota as she recorded all the songs for *The Runaways*, and complimented her on doing such a great job. Cherie also showed Dakota some of the moves she used to do on stage.

Vampire Guard

Dakota at the Los Angeles premiere of *Twilight: New Moon*.

The second of the *Twilight Saga* films, *Twilight: New Moon* was released in 2009. Dakota played Jane, one of the Volturi Guard.

Jane's special power is the ability to make people feel pain that's not really there. Fans used to Dakota playing the role of young girls were surprised at how compellingly wicked she was as a vampire. It was just another sign of her growing up.

During the
filming of *Twilight: New
Moon,* more than 5,000 of
Dakota's fans showed up in
the tiny Tuscan town
of Volterra.

THE NEXT CHAPTER BEGINS

the twilight saga
new moon

11.20.09

Dakota on a poster for the
movie *Twilight: New Moon.*

❝I wanted to be in
the film. I really
wanted to be a part
of the *Twilight
Saga,* even if it
was just a little
bit. It was really
exciting to get to be
a character in it ...
to get to have the
makeup and the
contact lenses and
the costumes was
really interesting.❞

Sweet Smell of Success

In 2011, the American fashion designer Marc Jacobs chose Dakota to be the face of his latest perfume, Oh, Lola! Marc made the decision shortly after seeing *The Runaways*. "I knew she could be this contemporary Lolita, seductive yet sweet," he said.

In the ads, Dakota wears a pink sundress and holds a large bottle of perfume. Top fashion photographer Juergen Teller shot the ads. However, some people thought Dakota looked too young to be advertising perfume in this way.

Dakota poses in front of the final ad for Oh, Lola!

"It's so weird shooting photos with [Juergen Teller], because he will take a few photos and then step back and you're like 'OK, I'll go with you.' It's not set-up poses. It's a fun day. There's no pressure to look a certain way or feel a certain way."

The ad for Oh, Lola!, featuring Dakota, was banned in the UK because some people thought it was too provocative.

Serious Student

During the early part of her career, Dakota didn't go to school. She had a tutor instead, who came with her whenever she was filming. Imagine having to do homework as well as learning all those lines!

Dakota didn't want to miss having a normal school life, though. She spent her teenage years at Campbell Hall School. She supported the school football team as a cheerleader, went to the school prom, and was even voted Homecoming Queen two years in a row! After graduating from high school in 2011, she attended New York University.

> **I'm homeschooled, and I have a teacher that goes with me on all my movies.**
> Dakota speaking in 2002

Dakota pulled out of the film *If I Stay* in order to concentrate on her studies in her final year at school.

Dakota graduated on June 6, 2011. The ceremony was held at the Walt Disney Hall in Los Angeles.

Moving On

Dakota went to college because she didn't want to miss having ordinary experiences. Ultimately, though, acting is the most important thing in her life. "It's cool to want to do this forever," she says.

Dakota had her hair cut short for her role in *Now Is Good* in 2012.

Dakota signs her autograph for waiting fans.

"I just feel so blessed to be able to [act], because it's unbelievable to work with these great actors that I have worked with, and I have all these friends that I've made on sets that I'll have all my life. That's the best part about it."

Br

After graduating from high school, Dakota began to take on acting work again. For the title role of the historical drama *Effie*, Dakota mastered a perfect English accent. Then in *Now Is Good*, she played the part of a girl dying of leukemia.

In the future, Dakota wants more varied roles so she can master new challenges. She recognizes that she can learn from others more experienced than she is. There are many actors with whom she'd love to work—Morgan Freeman is one, for example.

29

Fan Guide

Full Name: Hannah Dakota Fanning
Date of Birth: February 23, 1994
Height: 5 feet 4 inches (1.63 meters)
Hometown: Conyers, Georgia
Sun Sign: Pisces
Color of Eyes: Blue
Hobbies: Plays violin and piano, swimming

There are many, many sites about Dakota, and often they let you contribute to discussions about her. Remember, though, that it's OK to make comments, but it's not fair to be unkind. She cannot answer your comments herself!

http://dakota-fanning.org/

http://www.imdb.com/name/
nm0266824/

http://dfanningsource.com/

http://dakotafanningfan.com/

http://dakotafanningdaily.com/

http://www.hannahdakota
        fanning.com/

http://www.at-dakota.org/

http://hannahdakotafanning.info/

http://www.allmovieportal.com/
b/dakotafanning.html

http://www.nme.com/nme-video/
youtube/search/Dakota%20
Fanning

Please note: every effort has been made by the Publishers to ensure that these web sites contain no inappropriate or offensive material. However, because of the nature of the Internet, it is impossible to guarantee that the contents of these sites will not be altered. We strongly advise that Internet access is supervised by a responsible adult.

Feb 23, 1994	Hannah Dakota Fanning is born
1999	Moves to Los Angeles, California
	Stars in a detergent TV commercial
2000	Guest stars in *ER*'s "The Fastest Year" episode
	Appears in *Ally McBeal* as the young Ally
	Guest stars in *CSI: Crime Scene Investigation*
	Appears in *The Practice*'s "The Deal" episode
	Plays Cindy in *Spin City*'s "Toy Story" episode
2001	Appears as Marie in *The Fighting Fitzgeralds* pilot
	Plays Young Ellen on *The Ellen Show*
	Stars as Lucy Diamond Dawson in *I Am Sam*
2002	Wins Young Artist Award for *I Am Sam*
	Plays kidnap victim Abby Jennings in *Trapped*
	Appears in *Sweet Home Alabama* as the younger
	version of Reese Witherspoon's character
	Plays Katie in *Hansel and Gretel*
	Plays Allie Keys in Spielberg's miniseries, *Taken*
2003	Takes the role of Ray in *Uptown Girls*
	Stars in Dr. Seuss' *The Cat in the Hat*
	Voices Kim in *Kim Possible: A Stitch in Time*
2004	Guests in the *Friends* "Princess Consuela" episode
	Acts with Denzel Washington in *Man on Fire*
	Voices Young Wonder Woman in *Justice League*
2005	Plays Maria in *Nine Lives*
	Wins an MTV Movie Award for *Hide and Seek*
	Appears in *War of the Worlds* with Tom Cruise
	Voices Lilo in *Lilo and Stitch 2: Stitch Has a Glitch*
	Stars in *Dreamer: Inspired by a True Story*
2006	Wins Critics' Choice Award and Saturn Award for
	War of the Worlds
	Plays Fern Arable in *Charlotte's Web*
2007	Stars as Elvis Presley fan Lewellen in *Hounddog*
	Starts at Campbell Hall School
2008	Plays Lily Owens in *The Secret Life of Bees*
2009	Appears in the thriller *Push*
	Provides the voice for *Coraline*'s title character
	Plays Volturi Guard, Jane, in *Twilight: New Moon*
2010	Stars as Cherie Currie in *The Runaways*
	Appears in *Twilight: Eclipse*
2011	Graduates from high school
	Promotes Marc Jacobs' perfume, Oh, Lola!
	Enrolls at New York University
2012	Plays Tessa in *Now Is Good*
	Takes the title role in the costume drama *Effie*
	Plays Annie in *The Motel Life*
	Appears in *Twilight: Breaking Dawn—Part 2*

31

Glossary

Cast 1) The actors working on a movie or TV show. 2) Given a particular role.

Director The person in charge of making a movie or TV show.

Dramatization Turning a story into a play that can be acted on film or TV.

Improvise To make up words and actions instead of following a script.

Lolita The teenage girl character in Vladimir Nabokov's novel about a middle aged man's obsession with a teenage girl.

Miniseries A TV drama that tells a story over a set number of episodes.

Nominated To have one's name put forward for an award.

Pilot A sample episode, broadcast before committing to a whole series.

Premiere The first showing of a movie or TV show.

Producer The person who works with a director to make a film happen.

Index